Finders Keepers...

I Talk You Talk Press

CONTENTS

INTRODUCTION

"Finders keepers, losers weepers" is an English phrase.

It means "the person who finds something can keep it. The person who lost it cannot get the item back, so they are sad." (Weep = cry)

Do you agree with the phrase "Finders keepers, losers weepers"?

CHAPTER ONE

Jed Winters worked in a restaurant. He worked hard every day, but he didn't like his job. He started work at 11:00am and finished at 9:00pm. His salary was very low. He wanted to find a better job, but there were no other jobs in his town. He dreamed of a different life. He had no family. His father died before he was born. When he was born, his mother was very poor, and she couldn't keep Jed. He lived in a children's home until he was eighteen. Then, he started to work. He had no girlfriend. Every day, he went to work, and every night he went home, back to his small flat, and nothing changed.

Then, one day, something happened. Something that changed his life.

It was a cold and rainy day. Jed was on his way to work. He was waiting for the traffic lights to turn red on Sutton Road so he could cross over to the restaurant. He watched all the cars driving along the road.

I wish I had a car, he thought. He looked down at his feet. His shoes and socks were very wet. He hated walking in the rain. He noticed a small piece of paper next to his right foot. There were numbers on it.

He picked it up. The paper was very wet and dirty. He wiped it carefully with his sleeve and looked at it closely. It was a lottery ticket for the £500,000 lottery draw on Saturday.

He looked around, but he couldn't see anyone.

Someone has dropped a lottery ticket, he thought.

The traffic lights changed to red. He put the ticket in his pocket, crossed over the road and went into the restaurant.

The restaurant was very busy that day. Jed could not concentrate on his job. He couldn't stop thinking about the ticket.

The ticket is not mine. I shouldn't keep it. But whose is it? Who should I give it to? I didn't see anyone drop it. I was the only person at the traffic lights. If I keep the ticket, and if the ticket is a winner, I will be very rich, thought Jed. He started to dream.

I will have a big house and a big car. I will quit my job. I won't have to work for a long time. I will travel around the world…But no…I can't win! I never win anything! But this time…maybe…

That day, Jed made many mistakes with the customers' orders. His boss and the other waiters were angry with him.

"Jed! What's wrong with you today? Why are you making so many mistakes?" said Rob, another waiter. "What are you thinking about? Do you have a new girlfriend? Are you thinking about her?"

"No, I don't have a girlfriend. I'm sorry, Rob. Something happened this morning, and I can't stop thinking about it," said Jed.

"Something happened? Something bad?" asked Rob.

"I can't tell you," said Jed.

"Did you do something bad?" asked Rob.

"Yes, and no. I don't know," said Jed.

Jed went home that night and thought about it.

Did I do a bad thing? I found a lottery ticket on the ground. I picked it up. I put it in my pocket. That's not bad, thought Jed. *It isn't money. It's only a piece of paper with six numbers on it. And I probably won't win anything, so, it doesn't matter.*

Then, he remembered the famous English phrase "Finders Keepers, Losers Weepers."

Finders keepers, losers weepers…yes, that's right! I found it, so I keep it. The owner of the ticket lost it, so he or she weeps!

He put the ticket on his desk next to his computer and forgot about it.

CHAPTER TWO

The lottery draw was on Saturday evening. Jed worked very hard that day. There were many customers in the restaurant and he was busy from morning until night. He left the restaurant at 9:00pm and stopped at a supermarket to buy something to eat. He opened his wallet. He had very little money, and it was two weeks until pay day.

He used all of his money to repair the water heater system in his flat. His flat was very old and it had many problems. He didn't have enough money to buy a lot of food. He bought a frozen pizza and went home. He put the pizza in the oven.

Then he remembered the lottery ticket. He sat down at his desk and picked up the ticket.

He looked at the numbers.

2...14...15...32...35...38.

He switched his computer on and found the lottery ticket website. He clicked on the Saturday draw page. He looked at the numbers.

2...14...15...32...35...38.

He looked at the ticket again.

2...14...15...32...35...38.

Jed looked at the computer screen for a long time.

"This can't be right. There must be a mistake," he said. He looked at the ticket again. "No, there is a mistake," he said.

Then, he smelt a bad smell coming from the kitchen.

"Oh no! My pizza!"

He ran into the kitchen. There was smoke everywhere. He switched the oven off and opened the door. The smoke was very heavy. The pizza was burnt. It didn't look delicious, but Jed was very hungry. He put the pizza on a plate and went back to the computer.

He looked at the screen and the ticket again.

2…14…15…32…35…38.

"There's no mistake," he said.

"There's no mistake…I've…I've…I've won! I've won!"

Jed stood up and went to the window.

"I've won the lottery!" he screamed out of the window. "I've won the lottery! I've won half a million pounds!"

Jed couldn't believe it. He sat down on the floor and laughed for a long time. He was now a very rich man. He didn't have to worry about the problems in his flat anymore. He didn't have to buy cheap frozen pizza for dinner anymore. And he didn't have to work at the restaurant anymore.

He called his boss.

"Hello Mr. Hill, this is Jed," he said.

"Hi Jed. What's wrong?" said Mr. Hill. "It's very late. Are you OK?"

"I'm calling to tell you that I won't come to work tomorrow," said Jed.

"You won't come to work? What do you mean? We are always very busy on Sundays. You have to come to work!" said Mr. Hill.

"No, I don't have to come to work, because I quit! Goodbye!" said Jed. He put the phone down and started to laugh. That felt good!

"I always wanted to do that!" he said.

He started to eat the burnt pizza.

"This is the last time I eat cheap frozen pizza! From next week, I will eat at expensive restaurants and drink nice champagne every night! I will go shopping in the most expensive supermarkets. I can buy anything now!"

CHAPTER THREE

The lottery company paid the money into Jed's bank account. He looked at his bank book. Before, his bank account was minus £300. Now, it was £499,700.

Jed felt so happy, and so lucky.

The next week, he went on holiday to Monaco.

He felt good. It was very sunny every day. He spent his time shopping in expensive shops, gambling in casinos and relaxing in cafes, watching the rich and famous walking along the streets and driving expensive cars. There were rich people everywhere.

I am rich. I am like these people, he thought.

When he got home, he bought a new TV. He spent his days relaxing and having fun.

One day, he invited some friends to his flat for dinner.

Everyone was sitting in the dining room, eating food and drinking beer. They were having a good time.

"So, how could you afford to buy that TV?" asked his friend Sara.

"And how could you afford to quit your job at the restaurant?" asked his other friend Alain.

"An old aunt died. She left me some money," said Jed. He didn't want to tell his friends about the lottery ticket. So, he lied.

"Oh, I see," said Sara. "Your aunt was a very rich lady. How did she become so rich?"

"Oh, I don't know very well," said Jed. "I only met her once, when I was a child."

"Where did she live?" asked Sara.

"Oh, I think she lived in Ireland," said Jed.

"I see. How old was she?" asked Sara.

"I'm not sure. I think she was around ninety," said Jed.

"Are you going to work again?" asked Sara.

"Yes, I have to work in the future. But I'm not going to work until next year. I'm going on a trip around the world for a year," said Jed.

"Really? Wow! When will you leave?" asked Sara.

"Next week," said Jed.

"Is it very expensive?" asked Sara.

"Yes, it is. More beer, anyone?"

Jed didn't want to talk about the money. He went into the kitchen to get some more beer.

"Some people have money. Some people don't have money. That's life," said Alain. "Oh, Jed, did you see that story in the local newspaper?"

"What story?" asked Jed.

"The story about the woman with two children," said Alain.

"No, I didn't," said Jed.

He went into the living room and picked up the newspaper. "I haven't read it yet."

Alain opened the newspaper and read the story.

"A young mother and her two children have lost their home. The mother, Anna Walker, 23, could not pay the rent, and she had many debts. But did she win the lottery?

A debt collector went to the house last week and took Anna's sofa, table, chairs, and other items of furniture. He also took her TV and her children's toys.

The owner of the house told Anna to leave because she could not pay the rent. Now, she is living in a homeless shelter with her two children. She is on the waiting list for a council house, but there are many people on the list. She has to wait.

We interviewed Anna at the shelter.

She said, 'I want to do my best for my children. I have tried everything. A few months ago, I bought a lottery ticket for the £500,000 lottery with my last pound coin. I had a good feeling about the lottery that week. I was feeling very lucky. But then I dropped the lottery ticket on Sutton Road. I often think about that lottery ticket. Did someone find it? Did I win? I don't know.'

The workers at the homeless shelter are trying to help Anna to find a job, but there are not many jobs in the town. We hope Anna can get help soon."

Jed looked at the photograph of Anna and her children for a long time.

"Are you okay Jed?" asked Sara. "You look strange."

Jed didn't answer.

He thought about that day when he found the lottery ticket on Sutton Road. *It was Anna's ticket! She dropped it! And I kept it and spent the money! It's not my money! It's Anna's money! Anna has two children, but no job, no money and no house. Her children have no toys. I took her lottery ticket! I took her money!* he thought.

He opened another can of beer and drank it all. He felt very bad.

"It's a terrible story. I hope the woman and her children find happiness," said Alain.

"I'm going to buy her a lottery ticket. She probably won't win, but I hope she can!" said Sara.

"I'm going to buy her children some toys," said Alain.

Sara and Alain looked at Jed.

"Jed, you have money now. You could buy her children some toys too!" said Sara.

"Yeah, I will," said Jed. "OK, it's time for dessert! Wait a minute. I'll just go and get the cake."

Jed went into the kitchen and closed the door. He wanted to be alone.

I thought that I was in a bad situation. I didn't like my job, I didn't have much money. I dreamed of a nice car, and a nice house. I found the lottery ticket and kept it. I only thought about myself. I didn't think about the owner of the ticket. I'm a bad person, thought Jed.

The party finished and Jed's friends went home. Jed cleaned up and washed the dishes. All the time, he thought about the newspaper story. He thought about the woman and her children.

That night, Jed couldn't sleep. Every time he closed his eyes, he saw the faces of the two children. They were crying. He got up and made a cup of coffee.

What can I do? he thought. *I should give Anna the rest of the money. But no... finders keepers losers weepers...I should keep it. No, I should give her half the money...But why? Finders keepers...it's my money...*

Jed looked out of the window. The sun was starting to rise. As he watched the sun, he thought about his mother and his childhood.

My mother was poor. She couldn't keep me. I lost my mother. I lived in a children's home, with no family. I was very unhappy. And I'm sure my mother was very unhappy too.

Hot tears started to run from Jed's eyes down his face. He picked up the newspaper and looked at the photograph of Anna and her children. When he looked at the children, he saw his own face when he was a child.

I will take the money out of my account and give her the money! Yes! I will give her the money! he thought. *I don't want those children to grow up unhappy! I don't want them to grow up like me, with no mother or father, and no money!*

CHAPTER FOUR

The next morning, Jed went to his bank at 9:00am.

"Good morning Mr Winters, how can I help you today?" asked Mr Trimble, the bank manager.

"Could you tell me how much money I have left in my bank account, please?" asked Jed.

"Yes, of course. Just a moment please Mr Winters," said Mr Trimble. He looked at his computer.

Jed was nervous. How much money was left?

"You have £405,000 left," said Mr Trimble. "You bought a TV, then you went on a trip to Monaco, and next week, you will go on a trip around the world. You already paid your travel agent for that trip. It cost £70,000. You paid for that last week," said Mr Trimble. "And you bought some other things too."

"Yes, I did. Thank you," said Jed.

He stood up and walked out of the bank. It was cold and raining again. Yesterday, he was looking forward to going on the trip around the world. He wanted to see the sun and to relax on the beach. But now, he didn't want to go. He didn't want the money. It wasn't his money. It was Anna's money. He wanted to give it to her and her children. For Jed, that was now more important. He walked into the travel agency.

"Good morning Mr Winters," said the travel agent.

"Good morning," said Jed.

"Look at the rain! The weather is so bad. But you are very lucky! Next week, you will start your world cruise. You will go to many hot places! Lucky you!" said the travel agent.

"I'd like to cancel my trip," said Jed.

"Cancel your trip? Why?" the travel agent asked.

"Something happened. I can't go. Can I have a refund please?" asked Jed.

"A refund? Yes, we can give you your money back, but, we have to take a cancellation fee," said the travel agent.

"How much is the cancellation fee?" asked Jed.

"It's £10,000," said the travel agent.

"So I can get £60,000 back?" asked Jed.

"Yes, that's right," said the travel agent.

"When can you give me the money?"

"We can put the money into your bank account today," said the travel agent.

"OK, thank you," said Jed.

£405,000 plus £60,000 equals £465,000 thought Jed. *I only spent around £35,000. That's not so much really.*

He left the travel agency and went to a café. He ordered a cup of coffee and sat at a table next to the window. He watched the rain outside.

How can I give Anna the money? If I try to give it to her, she will ask, 'Where did you get the money?' he thought. I don't want to lie, but I don't want to tell her about the lottery ticket. She will say 'You stole my money!' She might tell the newspapers. My friends will be very disappointed. I will never find another job. So, how can I give her the money? What can I do?

Jed sat in the café and thought about the problem for many hours. Then, he had an idea.

CHAPTER FIVE

The next morning, Jed got up at 7:00am. It was a bright sunny morning. He left the house at 8:00am and walked to the homeless shelter. He stood across the road from the homeless shelter and watched the entrance. He waited for Anna.

At 8:15 she came out with her children. The youngest child, a boy, was crying. Anna and her children looked very sad. Jed felt bad when he saw them. He followed them up the hill. They went into the school. He waited across the road from the school. There were many mothers, fathers and children. Five minutes later, Anna and her son came out of the school and they walked back down the hill. Then, they went into a small supermarket. Jed followed them. The boy stopped at the chocolate section.

"Mummy! I want this chocolate!" he said.

Anna looked very sad.

"I know. But we have no money for chocolate. We need to buy some bread."

Jed looked at the chocolate bar. It was very cheap. It was only thirty pence. She didn't even have thirty pence to buy chocolate. Jed felt even worse.

Anna bought a small loaf of bread, and left the shop. Jed followed her and her son. They went into the park and walked to the play area. The boy smiled. He ran to the swings and sat on a swing. Anna put her shopping bags on a bench behind her. Then, she pushed her son on the swing. Jed stood behind a tree and watched them.

"Mummy, when we get a house, I want a garden with a swing,"

said the child.

Anna looked sad.

"Can we have a garden with a swing?" asked the child.

Jed watched Anna. There were tears in her eyes.

"Please mummy? When can we get a house? When can we have a garden?"

Tears fell down Anna's face.

"I don't know, Joe," said Anna.

"Promise me, mummy, promise me that we can have a garden," said the boy.

"I promise," whispered Anna.

Jed felt so bad when he heard this.

Then, after half an hour, Anna and her son went to the lake. The lake in the park was very big. There were many ducks in the lake.

"Mummy, the ducks are hungry," said Joe. "Can we give the ducks some bread?"

"No Joe," said Anna. "If we give the ducks some bread, we won't have anything to eat today. You will be hungry, too. We need that bread for dinner tonight."

They are only eating bread for dinner?! thought Jed. *That's terrible!*

Jed went home and thought about his plan. He wanted to help Anna and her children soon. But he decided to wait a few more days. He wanted to know her daily schedule.

The next day, he did the same thing. He went to the shelter at 8:00am and watched the entrance. Anna and her children came out at 8:15 and they walked up to the school. Then, Anna and her youngest child went to the small supermarket, and then they went to the park. After that, they walked back to the shelter.

Every day, Jed followed them. They did the same thing every day. Now, he knew their schedule. It was time to give Anna the money.

CHAPTER SIX

The next day, Jed went to his bank to talk to Mr Trimble.

"I'd like to take out all the money in my account," said Jed.

"Are you serious?" asked Mr Trimble.

"Yes, I am. I want the money in cash. Please put it in this bag," said Jed.

"Mr Winters, it is very dangerous to carry so much money. Are you in trouble? Has something bad happened?"

"No. I'm not in trouble. I just want my money. I'm going to buy something in cash," said Jed.

"Mr Winters, £405,000 is a lot of money. We cannot let you take that much cash. Please pay by bank transfer or credit card. It is much safer," said Mr Trimble.

"No. I want the cash! And it's not £405,000. It's £465,000. I cancelled my trip. It's my money! You have to give me it! Please take the money out of my account and put it in this bag," said Jed. "Now! Now! If you don't, I will never use this bank again! Do it now!"

"Okay, Mr Winters. Please wait a moment," said Mr Trimble. He was very worried, but Jed was very angry. He decided to give Jed the money.

An hour later, Jed left the bank with £465,000 in cash. It was very heavy. He went home and hid the money under his bed. Then, he went to a shop and bought a cap and sunglasses. That night, he thought about his plan.

I will sit in the park near the children's play area. I will wear the cap and sunglasses so people can't see my face. Anna always leaves her shopping bag on the bench when her son is on the swing. When they are at the swings, I will put the money next to her shopping bag, and then I will run away. It's a great plan!

Then, he took a paper and pen from his desk and wrote a message on the paper:

This money is for you and your family. Please buy a house with a garden and a swing. Your family will be happy there.

Then, he put the message in the bag with the money. The bag was strong, but it didn't have a lock. It only had a zip.

Is this bag strong enough? Should I use a box? thought Jed.

He looked around his house, but he couldn't find a suitable box. He decided to use the bag. Then, he opened a bottle of wine.

How will I live? he thought. *I need to get a job quickly. I can't call my old boss at the restaurant. He won't give me a job. I'll go to the job centre tomorrow after giving Anna the money. I'll be fine. And Anna and her children will have a good life. And, it isn't all bad. I had a nice time in Monaco, and I have a new TV.*

Jed soon fell asleep on the sofa.

In his dream, he saw Anna's children playing in a garden. In the garden there was a swing, and the children were happy.

Then, something strange happened.

The little boy suddenly started shouting.

"Mummy! Mummy!"

"What is it?" said Anna. She ran into the garden.

"It's raining money!" he said. "Money is falling from the sky!"

Anna walked out into the garden. She looked up at the sky. Money was falling down into the garden. Anna and her children started laughing. They tried to pick up the money, but when they touched the money, it disappeared, and the children started to cry.

CHAPTER SEVEN

Jed opened his eyes.

That was a strange dream, he thought.

He looked at the clock on the wall.

"8:30!! Oh no! I've overslept! I'm going to be late!" he said.

Jed got dressed very quickly and brushed his teeth. Then he put on his cap and sunglasses. He grabbed the bag of money and ran out of the door. He didn't notice that the bag was open.

Jed ran through the streets. There were many cars and many people. Some people looked at him. He looked strange. It was a very cloudy day, but he was wearing a cap and sunglasses. And he was carrying a heavy bag and running.

It was also a very windy day. Jed ran against the wind into the park.

I have to give Anna the money! I have to give Anna the money! he thought.

He didn't notice some of the money falling out of his bag.

He didn't see the banknotes flying away behind him in the sky.

He didn't see the money and his message falling into the lake.

He didn't see the hungry ducks trying to eat the fifty pound notes.

He didn't see the people behind him, picking up the banknotes.

He didn't hear a man shout, "Look! It's raining money! Money is falling from the sky!" He didn't hear a woman shout, "A man wearing sunglasses and a cap is running with a big bag of money! He looks like a bank robber! Call the police!"

He only thought about giving the money to Anna.

He arrived at the play area. Anna and her son were at the swings.

Her shopping bag was on the bench. Jed relaxed and stopped running. He walked slowly over to the bench. Anna didn't see him. She was talking to her son.

He looked down at his bag, and shouted, "Oh no! The money! Some of it has gone!"

Anna and her son turned around and looked at him.

"Are you OK?" asked Anna.

Jed looked at her face. Their eyes met, and he panicked.

He threw the bag down on the ground and ran away. He didn't want Anna to see his face. He could hear people behind him. They were shouting, "Stop! Stop!"

Anna picked up the bag and opened it.

"It's money!" she said. "That man dropped all this money and ran away! Why? Is he a bank robber?"

Then, she saw a policewoman running towards her.

"Excuse me, did you see a man wearing sunglasses and a cap?" asked the policewoman.

"Yes, I did. He dropped this money," said Anna.

"Oh, you are very honest," said the policewoman. "Many people saw the money and picked it up and kept it."

"I don't think that's right. The money is not mine. Is he a bank robber?"

"I don't think so," said the policewoman. "We checked all the banks. They are all fine."

"Well, this is the man's money. I hope you find him. If you find him give the money back to him," said Anna.

"Can I have your name and address please?" asked the policewoman.

"Yes, of course. My name is Anna Walker. My address is…well…actually…I don't have an address. I'm homeless. I live in the homeless shelter with my children," said Anna.

"Oh, I see," said the policewoman. She wrote down Anna's name and information in her notebook.

Jed ran into the bushes next to the lake. He was very tired and he couldn't breathe. He saw the policewoman run past. She didn't see him. Then, he saw Anna and her son. They stopped at the lake.

"Look mummy! Look! The ducks are eating money!" said Anna's son. "The man will be hungry. He lost his money, so he can't buy bread. But today, the ducks are lucky. Usually, they don't have any bread to eat, but today, they can eat the money. They won't be hungry anymore. And, we won't be hungry today because we have bread. We are very lucky."

"Yes, that's right," said Anna. "The ducks are very lucky. Just like us."

Jed watched Anna and her son as they walked out of the park.

He thought about the day when he picked up the lottery ticket.

That day, I thought "finders keepers, losers weepers" was a good phrase. But, now, I don't think so, thought Jed.

He went home and started looking for a new job.

A few months later, he moved to London and found a job in a restaurant. He tried to forget about the money and Anna.

Six months later, the policewoman went to the homeless shelter.

She said to the manager, "Can I see Ms Walker, please?"

"Yes, just a moment," said the manager.

A few minutes later, Anna Walker came to the entrance.

"Hello Ms Walker. I have some news for you," said the policewoman.

"News for me? What?" asked Anna.

"Do you remember a man dropping money in the park a few months ago?" asked the policewoman.

"Yes, I do," said Anna.

"Well, we kept the money in the police station, but six months have passed, and no one came to get the money," said the policewoman. "So, because you found the money and gave it to the police, you can have the money."

"Pardon? I don't understand," said Anna.

"You found the money, so you can have it Ms Walker! There was £452,000 in the bag. You can keep it!" said the policewoman.

"Really? But, but..." Anna was very surprised. "It's not my money! I can't take it!"

"Of course you can take it!" said the policewoman. "Take it. It's yours. Give your children a happy life. Finders keepers, losers weepers!"

Anna laughed. "Yes! I always thought 'finders keepers, losers weepers' was a bad phrase. But, now...now I don't think it's so bad! Thank you! Thank you so much!"

THANK YOU

Thank you for reading Finders Keepers…! We hope you enjoyed Jed's story. (Word count: 4,964)

There are quizzes about this book on our free study site I Talk You Talk Press EXTRA. http://italk-youtalk.com

If you would like to read more graded readers, please visit our website
http://www.italkyoutalk.com

Other Level 2 graded readers include
Adventure in Rome
Andre's Dream
A Passion for Music
Christmas Tales
Danger in Seattle
Don't Come Back
Marcy's Bakery
Men's Konkatsu Tales
Salaryman Secrets!
Stories for Halloween
The Perfect Wedding
The House in the Forest
The School on Bolt Street
Train Travel

Trouble in Paris
Women's Konkatsu Tales

ABOUT THE AUTHOR

I Talk You Talk Press is a Japan-based publisher of language textbooks, graded readers and language learning/teaching resources.

Our team is made up of highly experienced language teachers and translators, who have all studied at least one additional language to an advanced level.

This experience enables us to design our materials from the perspective of both the teacher and the learner. We consult with both teachers and language learners when designing our textbooks and graded readers, and test our materials extensively in the classroom before publication.

We are a fast-growing press, and currently publish graded readers for learners of English. We publish new graded readers monthly.

www.ingramcontent.com/pod-product-compliance
Lightning Source LLC
Chambersburg PA
CBHW022352040426
42449CB00006B/850